21

Poetry

Stevie Bre

BookLeaf Publishing

India | USA | UK

Made with ❤ on the BookLeaf Publishing Platform
www.bookleafpub.in
www.bookleafpub.com

Dedication

This book is dedicated to the past me. For always wanting more for my writing and actually pursuing something.

Preface

These Poems are all about feelings and sorts of brain
dumps.

Acknowledgements

Forever grateful to my friends and family who have been here encouraging me

1. Loss

I can't for a moment
Put myself in your shoes
What would I say
Or do
What would I feel
How would I choose to live out my last moments
I can't begin to even think of how you feel
But I'm asking all these questions
Trying to learn how to deal
How my heart aches to see your pain
How I mourn your loss
Their loss
My loss
I can't for a moment understand
Where would I be
How would I tell them
What would they want
What do you want
For a moment, I try
To think what you think
Only a tear falls
Not even for a moment
Could I understand how it feels
To live only to know you're dying

To try each day to keep going
The body knowing
The symptoms showing
Eyes sinking in
Heart slowing down
Body aches
But you push on
And for a moment longer
You live
And for that moment
We hold On

2. Feelings

Not sure why or how
But there is something there
Whenever you are near me I stumble
Almost fall
Seem to catch myself
But look like a fool
How do I demonstrate
How much I like you
Without being a fool
How do I stay true
To being authentically me
When I am afraid that might frighten you
You are the reason I lie to myself
Like my anxiety
You make me feel as though I may not be good enough
If this is the case then maybe you're no good for me

So here I sit wondering what you might think of me
In realizations knowing it shouldn't matter
In my strength I see myself powerful
Around you I feel weak

In the knees
My brain fumbles on silly words
And sometimes just stops
I stare and realize you've caught me
Romanticizing the entire moment
Even though its hard to even look directly at you
Intimidating yet exhilarating
And focus is completely lost
If only I could just say what was on my mind
If you could just read the thoughts and know I am not
some psychotic love crazed person
Or maybe I am
But you make everything slip away
So I stay in this moment

3. Lost

I want to get lost in conversations
To feel like I am in another world
To hold someone's hand
Walk down a street and laugh
Try new things and write it all down
Love endlessly
I want to get lost in the stars
Laying under the vast sky
Caring only about the moment
Wondering what stars are falling
and should I make a wish
I should be lost in your eyes
In your words, you speak
Should be lost in the warmth of your energy
Lost in your touch
That's where I want to be
Lost in conversation with just you

4. Romatasize

I want to romanticize every aspect of my life.
To think how amazing it is to sit in the sunlight
To breath
To walk
Romanticize the way I talk
The words that spill from my tongue
Brushing slightly against my lips
Full and bursting with life
Romanticize the things I see
The world around me
Bustling and loud
But beautiful in every sense of the word
Seeing all the people
Knowing they all love someone or something
Thinking of the way they long for their partners to touch
Thinking of how some are just falling in love
Some are walking into new lives
And it's all romantic
It's all chaotically pleasing
To know you're out there
Maybe thinking of me
Maybe romanticizing the moments we share
Waiting for our next moment
I like to romanticize the very thought of being romantic

To beautify the world around me
To look at things a bit differently

5. untitled

There was a moment
Between our souls
A flicker of light beyond our control
Moving towards it
Hearts pounding
So loudly our ears rang
Forever to keep this moment
But we can't and oh it's such a shame
The rapture we so badly desired
And yet I don't even know your name
But can feel the desire
Deep within my veins
Pumping harder between my legs
Warmth rushing to all the right places
A rosy red red-cheeked smile splashed across your face
You part your lips and whisper
"You're beautiful."
Suddenly, the door opens
People rush about
and you're now on the other side
And that moment rushes away

Whispers soft

Skin hyper-aware
Lip checking
Hands caressing
Hearts pounding
Intense rushes
Nerves soften
Breathing in
Breathing out
Lips connect
Heart races
Soul sores
Kissing
Touching
Exploring
Wanting more

6. Tease

Wishing I knew why I wanted you so badly
How do you tease me
And not even know
Or maybe you do know.
Maybe you have a way of keeping a hold of me
Casting a spell
The magic you hold
Makes me comfortable
Feeling safe
And wanting you so much more
When will I see you again
I never know
I'm having a hard time containing this desire
I want to text you
I want you to call

7. Rambles

The light was a warm glow
Touching across the leaves
Lighting the path
Across our bodies
Like my fingers trace your skin
Diving deeper into you
Loving the shadow play
Kisses across the light
The light that dances across
Your skin
Like my lips
Craving to dance across yours
A deepening desire
Reaching my core

There was so much to say but words were not exchanged
The language spoken between breaths
Was spoken with touch
Skin warm with lustful blood pumping through their
veins
The soft breaths turning into heavy hums
Moans and gasps as fingers slide effortlessly across her
breasts

Her heart beating fast as she touches his hips
Hands traveling caressing each other
He kisses her neck
And she shivers with pleasure
She reaches for his sex
And he teases and pulls away
She is eager to feel him
But he wants her to wait
To build the anticipation
To be in sync with how long they have wanted each
other
His hands glide to her breasts
As he cups them and whispers in her ear
"I want to make you wet"
She sighs and pulls his body close to her
From behind she can feel him
Hard and warm
She shakes with vulnerability
She wants to take him now

8. Dust of Old Bones

In that instant, I felt alone
The moment I knew would certainly come,
my hopes had faded as I searched,
but nothing at all would be unearthed,
I closed my eyes
hands digging deep
Suddenly, there was no ground
no feeling
I opened my eyes, but darkness surrounded me
I blinked in confusion; there was now nothing around
me
Then a thud thud crumble
My heart it should be racing
somehow I was unbothered
 I reached out and grasped into the empty abyss. surely,
there should be something here
 But alas, there was only a mist light and airy
 Then a foul smell
realization rotting flesh?
I fumbled in the darkness
Flashing my lighter on
there in the dim light
I realized where I'd gone
 all around me, the darkness grew

and at that moment I knew
I was there
buried alive amongst the dust of old bones

9. She Craves

The way she craves to touch
To explore
To watch how his body reacts
Her eyes follow his
To connect deeply
Knowing what she wants
And him letting her take it
She craves to taste his skin on her lips
His hands gripping her hips
Her hands all over his body
His desire growing
Hers overflowing
She craves to devour him
To let her intentions clearly known
She craves everything about him

10. Past Shell

What was it that made me feel so unworthy
The comparing game
The need and want to fit in
To be a size 00
How come I didn't feel like I would be loved if I had a
little bit of a love handles
The thought of how much I gave up
To be something you'd want
And still, you didn't want me
I gave up so much time and energy
To fulfill a life I'd never actually see
But somehow someone always wanted something from
me
And they didn't ask
They just took
And when someone finally saw me for me
And held my hand
And told me how sorry they were that I had to endure
that kind of pain
That person told me unfortunately, they went through
the same thing
They endured sleepless nights
Panic attacks
And nightmares they could never outrun

They sat with me and let me spill my story out
Until I felt like I was done
But they told me with time it would flood back
Bit by bit and year by year, it would always be different
At some point, you barely recognize the reason the pain
is swelling in your chest
Til a song plays or a smell reminds you of the pain you
endured
You learn to recognize the cues from your body
Remind yourself to breathe
You gather strength from listing gratitudes
And being amazed you're still moving forward

When you look back and see that young woman who
could barely stand to live you
Hold out your hands to her and remind her it's all worth
it in the end.

11. 8/19/24

She was something else
Not like anyone
Something you'd think was a dream
Her conscience concepts
The way she addressed moments
Her knack to know how to calm you
The look in her eyes when she found something she
needed and wanted. Her tactics to gain attention
The moments she made you feel
Alive
She was something.
Something you'd have to learn to miss
She was done waiting
Done hoping you'd give her the attention she desired
So she walked away
Found the things in life that made her know
That she is something special
Something Seductive and something no one else could
be
She knows her worth
She deserves so much more

12. Don't I

I have to let you go though
Don't I

I have to say goodbye to the hope
That I'll ever have a moment with you
The connection with you that once was

I have to let it all go
Don't I

The moment I met you
The feelings I felt
And tried to ignore
Because something was telling me
I'd have to let you go
Just as soon as I thought I had you

I have to let it all go
Don't I

The memories build
In the blink of an eye
The moments we held each other
The one time I truly saw you for you

Better to let the memories all die
Because I have to let you go

Don't I.

13. To Tell You

I feel like if I told you all the things I've wanted to
you would look at me and think I was dumb
You'd say I was wasting my breath
Tell me there's no point
The anxiety that sits in my chest
Would explode
And leave me empty
Maybe that's what I need
To express these feelings
Make room for the void
The way you feel for me
is nothing
And I should know better than to have thought anything
other
Breaking this habit
This pattern
Addicted
I'm finally seeing it and admitting
To you, my love
And you have yet to hear it truly
You've felt it
But never actually acknowledged
And these thoughts and feelings will stay within me

Leaving me feeling anxious
But trying to stay numb

14. Engaged in You

Sudden pulling of my strings
Has me begging
Back on my knees
Thought I was over
Now just overwhelmed
But the haunting sensations
Wanting to feel
To touch
To taste
But knowing this isn't your subtly
Fully engaged
Only I can see
You're not here to be with me
Only a placeholder
That's all I'll be
But here I am still begging
Wanting you to be with me

15. 3 Words

Simple 3 words
That make the world
For some
And leave others feeling alone
3 words
Strung together
Hoping to hold truth
At least when spoken
To one another
Simple
But not
3 words
I like you
No
3 words
I love you
Simple?
Love is never simple
And loving you is all I ever want

16. Big Feels

I'm not sure the world understands
My heart and feelings
Don't match the social dealings
I'm naive to some
And others I am insane
Why would I love more
Than just one person
Why would I engage in life
In such a non traditional way
It's ok to be misunderstood
I'm not hurting anyone
And I'm not pushing to change the world
Just learning to enhance this life
One amazing friendship
Or situationship at a time
I'm not sure I want to be understood
My heart and feeling
Are bigger than this world

17. Alone

Alone
Yet Not
Abandonded
With everyone still around
Floating on mindlessly
Disappearing suddenly
Find me there
Alone

18. In Between

It's in the moments
In between
I get lost in overthinking
Over planning
Over analyzing
In the moment
I am immersed
So blissful and fully
I take it in
Full detail
Holding to every feeling
Raw emotion
Constant wonder
Holding to the present
Staying away from overthinking the future
Not looking to the past
And in the moments between
I unravel
Find myself hopelessly floundering
To make sense of who I once was
Who I am now
and who I want to be.

19. End of Day

Every moment felt fleeting
As the tie on the clock kept repeating
Hour by hour
Minute by minute
Eventually revealing the day has a limit
Crashing
Falling
Dwindling to nothing
Rays of light disapear
and Darkness develops
Wandering through the mind
Plays tricks
As nighttime takes on
Like an evil witch
Which dreams will grace the mind
Evil
or Sweet
Maybe we would rather not sleep

20. Truth

There it is
The truth
Strung out in front of the world
The light and shadow
The depths of my soul
I'm bearing it all
For the sake of not carrying it anymore
It's heavy.
Tears my heart to shreds
Makes others who hear about it
shake and hang their heads
But this is me
FULLY
showing my cracks and flaws
Letting the sun show the heartaches that I have caused
The truth is
I still love just as hard as the day I fell
The truth is
The walls I have built will be moved with just one word
Truth
is
I
Am
Human

21. Keeper

A keeper of hearts,
I loan my soul, mind, body to those who need a safe space
To hold them close help them mend
Move them into their deepest desires
To only have to let them go
When they move to their next
I crave to have a safe space in them as well
They seem to be there but then pull away
When they see what's pulling them
I am entangled with my own dark side
The side that wants and desires to do unchained things
To go off the rails and seek thrills
And somehow those thrills are filled with others' desire to be with me
Connecting to and breathing in the life of someone I never knew I'd be
Multiple lovers and multiple lives to lead
Open-hearted and navigating a world so cold
But I am a keeper of hearts, a lover of each soul
To know them is to love them
And to Love them is to let them go
It's never easy, and I feel their angst
The way they know I am only temporary

They can't hold me forever
Can't stay the night
Won't wake up next to me
Or kiss me whenever they feel
I see the pain that comes with loving someone like me
And I feel the way they keep themselves at bay
Never going too deep
They see I will keep their heart safe
As they learn to grow and understand their own needs
And wander to seek their own
A keeper of hearts I know it's not the best way
But it's a way to love unlimited
A way to pour myself out
Try and not fall
Try not to be too involved
Only here temporarily
Loving from a safe distance
Just a keeper of hearts